P9-BZC-271

The Bald Eagle

Tristan Boyer Binns

Heinemann Library
Chicago, Illinois

McLEAN COUNTY UNIT #5
105-CARLOCK

© 2001 Reed Educational & Professional Publishing
Published by Heinemann Library,
an imprint of Reed Educational & Professional Publishing,
Chicago, IL

Customer Service 888-454-2279

Visit our website at www.heinemannlibrary.com

All rights reserved. No part of this publication may be reproduced or transmitted in any form or by any means, electronic or mechanical, including photocopying, recording, taping, or any information storage and retrieval system, without permission in writing from the publisher.

Designed by Lisa Buckley
Illustration by David Westerfield
Printed in Hong Kong

05 04 03 02 01
10 9 8 7 6 5 4 3 2 1

Library of Congress Cataloging-in-Publication Data
Binns, Tristan Boyer, 1968-
    The Bald Eagle / Tristan Boyer Binns.
        p. cm. -- (Symbols of freedom)
    Includes bibliographical references (p.) and index.
    ISBN 1-58810-118-5 (lib. bdg.)   ISBN 1-58810-402-8 (pbk. bdg.)
        1. United States--Seal--Juvenile literature. 2. Bald eagle--United States--Juvenile
    literature. 3. Emblems, National--United States--Juvenile literature. 4. Signs and
    symbols--United States-Juvenile literature. [1. United States--Seal. 2. Emblems,
    National. 3. Signs and symbols. 4. Bald eagle. 5. Eagles.] I. Title.

CD5610 .B56 2001
929.9--dc21
                                                                    00-058138

Acknowledgments
The author and publishers are grateful to the following for permission to reproduce copyright material: p.4-5, 22 Chase Swift/Corbis, p.6 Alex Bee/Corbis, p.7 Bob Daemerich/Stock, Boston/PictureQuest, p.8 Joseph Sohm/Corbis, p.9, 11 Bettemann/Corbis, p.10 Library of Congress, p.12 Mark Downey/Lucid Images/PictureQuest, p.13 AP Photo, p.14 Chuck Fishman/Contact Press/PictureQuest, p.15 Joseph Sohm/ChromoSohm/Stock Connection/PictureQuest, p.16, 24 Bettemann/Corbis, p.17 Francis G. Mayer/Corbis, p.18 Mary Ann McDonald/Corbis, p.19 National Archives, p.20 Corbis, p.21 New York Historical Society [neg. #22650], p.23 Paul Souders/Corbis, p.26 Joel Bennett/Corbis, p.27 Reuters NewMedia Inc./Corbis, p.28 Ron Watts/Corbis, p.29 Farrell Grehan/Corbis.
Cover photograph courtesy of The White House.

Every effort has been made to contact copyright holders of any material reproduced in this book. Any omissions will be rectified in subsequent printings if notice is given to the publisher.

Some words are shown in bold, **like this.**
You can find out what they mean by looking in the glossary.

Contents

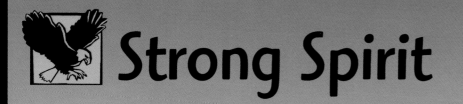 Strong Spirit

The eagle is a **symbol** of the United States.
It stands for strength, peace, and freedom.

Bald eagles only live in **North America.**
Many people think that the bald eagle shows
the **spirit** of the American people.

Eagles All Around Us

The bald eagle was first used on a gold coin more than 200 years ago. It is still on coins and dollar bills.

There are eagle statues at the tops of flagpoles. There is an eagle on every button of a **military officer's** uniform. The eagle has been a **logo** on the uniforms of government workers.

# The Great Seal

The Great **Seal** of the United States has
a bald eagle on it. The Great Seal is stamped
on important government papers. This shows
that the paper is **official.**

The eagle on the seal holds an olive branch in one foot. It means that the United States wants peace. There are arrows in the other foot. This means that the United States is ready to fight if it has to.

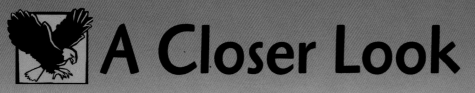

A Closer Look

The bald eagle on the Great **Seal** has a **shield** on its chest. It shows that the United States can **protect** itself. The stripes on the shield stand for the thirteen original states.

The eagle is holding a ribbon in its mouth. The words on the ribbon are in **Latin.** They mean "One out of many." All fifty states together make one United States of America.

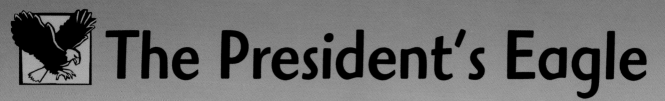# The President's Eagle

The eagle stands for the president of the United States, too. The president has a **seal** called the "presidential seal." It looks a lot like the Great Seal.

There is a bald eagle on the carpet in the president's office in the **White House.** Even the candies on the president's airplane have bald eagles on them!

A New Look

The presidential **seal** has not always looked the way it does today. Today, there are 50 stars around the eagle. They stand for the 50 states.

At one time, the eagle on the seal looked toward the arrows in its foot. President Harry Truman thought this was too warlike. In 1945, he changed the seal so that the eagle looks toward the olive branch.

On July 4, 1776, the United States became an **independent** country. The **founders** of the United States decided that the new country needed a Great **Seal.**

16

Benjamin Franklin, John Adams, and Thomas Jefferson helped with the design for the Great Seal. They had a lot of ideas, but no one could agree on one.

Eagle or Turkey?

Six years went by. Some people thought the Great **Seal** should show a bald eagle. But Benjamin Franklin wanted a turkey. He thought it was a truly American bird.

At last, everyone decided on the bald eagle. A man named Charles Thomson drew the design in one week. This is his drawing for the Great Seal of the United States.

The First President

George Washington became the first president
of the United States in 1789. He was **sworn in**
under the new American **symbol,** the bald
eagle. His suit buttons had bald eagles on them.

People all over America celebrated. They wanted to show their **patriotism.** So some of their fans, handkerchiefs, and buttons had bald eagles on them.

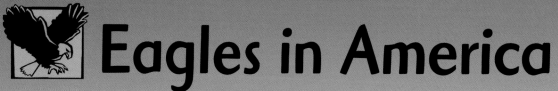

Eagles in America

When the first **settlers** came to America, bald eagles lived almost everywhere in the country. They had lived there for at least a million years.

People built homes, farms, and businesses
in places where eagles lived. After 100 years,
bald eagles were dying out.

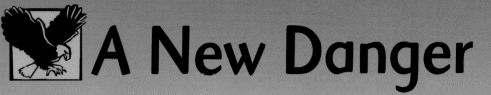 # A New Danger

By 1940 there were a lot fewer bald eagles.
A law called the Bald Eagle Act helped eagles.
People were not allowed to hurt or kill them.
But a new danger came from a spray called DDT.

DDT was a poison that killed insects. Bald eagles ate animals that had eaten the dead insects. The poison made the eagles sick.

Solving Problems

People saw that all the bald eagles would soon be dead. **Congress** helped by making more laws to **protect** bald eagles. The use of DDT was **outlawed.**

It took nearly 30 years to help the bald eagles recover. People still have to help bald eagles. But the future looks bright for this national **symbol.**

 Native American Symbol

Before the bald eagle became the **symbol** of the United States, Native Americans thought it was important. Some Native American tribes named themselves after the bald eagle.

Many Native American tribes used the bald eagle's feathers to show that a person had done something brave. Feathers were also used in **ceremonies.** They were signs of peace.

Bald Eagle

The Presidential **Seal** is called a "die." There have been seven dies since the first one was made in 1782.

The stars were added to the Presidential Seal in 1945 to show that the president is chosen by all of the people in the states. In 1945, there were 48 stars because there were 48 states.

Everything on the Great Seal is arranged in groups of thirteen.

- ⭐ 13 stripes in the **shield**
- ⭐ 13 arrows in the eagle's foot
- ⭐ 13 stars above the eagle's head